Skills Builders

Times Tables

1, 2, 5 AND 10

Hilary Koll and Steve Mills

RISING STARS

Rising Stars UK Ltd, 7 Hatchers Mews, Bermondsey Street, London SE1 3GS
www.risingstars-uk.com

Every effort has been made to trace copyright holders and obtain their permission for the use of copyright materials. The publishers will gladly receive information enabling them to rectify any error or omission in subsequent editions.

All facts are correct at time of going to press.

Published 2013
Reprinted 2014
Text, design and layout © 2013 Rising Stars UK Ltd

Project manager: Dawn Booth
Editorial: Roanne Charles
Proofreader: Jane Jackson
Illustrator: Dave Thompson
Design: Words & Pictures Ltd, London
Cover design: Amina Dudhia

British Library Cataloguing-in-Publication Data
A CIP record for this book is available from the British Library.

ISBN: 978-0-85769-686-1
Printed in Singapore by Craft Print International

1, 2, 5 AND 10

Contents

How to use this book

What we have included:

- Each unit covers aspects of the multiplication and division facts related to the 1, 2, 5 and 10 times tables.

- Each unit provides opportunity to practise recalling the number facts in and out of order. You can time yourself to see how you are progressing.

- We have included questions that involve a range of mathematical vocabulary, such as product, shared between, divided by, multiple and so on.

- There are three sections of word problems to ensure that you can use your times tables and division facts in many different contexts.

- All answers are included so you can check your progress.

1 — Some units begin with a useful tip to help you work out answers to the questions more quickly.

2 — **Test 1** involves answering the facts from the times table, usually presented in order. This helps you to see what the unit is about and what you must memorise.

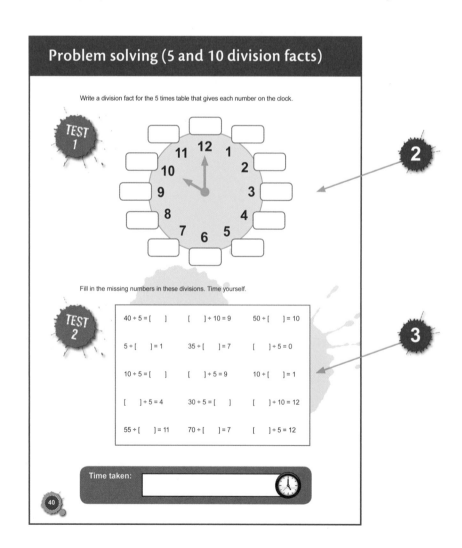

Problem solving (5 and 10 division facts)

Write a division fact for the 5 times table that gives each number on the clock.

TEST 1

2

Fill in the missing numbers in these divisions. Time yourself.

TEST 2

40 ÷ 5 = [   ]   [   ] ÷ 10 = 9   50 ÷ [   ] = 10

5 ÷ [   ] = 1   35 ÷ [   ] = 7   [   ] ÷ 5 = 0

10 ÷ 5 = [   ]   [   ] ÷ 5 = 9   10 ÷ [   ] = 1

[   ] ÷ 5 = 4   30 ÷ 5 = [   ]   [   ] ÷ 10 = 12

55 ÷ [   ] = 11   70 ÷ [   ] = 7   [   ] ÷ 5 = 12

3

Time taken:

40

How to use this book

3   **Test 2** gives similar questions but usually in a different order to make sure you learn them in any order. You can also time yourself to see how quickly you can answer them.

4   **Warming up** – This section is based on the same number facts as the tests but are presented in words, using mathematical language you should know.

5   **Getting hotter** – This section involves word problems. You'll need to use the facts you are learning to answer them. Read them very carefully.

6   **Burn it up** – This section has even more challenging questions and problems. You'll need to think very carefully and read each question several times to make sure you reach the correct answer.

7   **How did I do?** This gives you a chance to show how confident you feel about the number facts and to say how well you think you are doing.

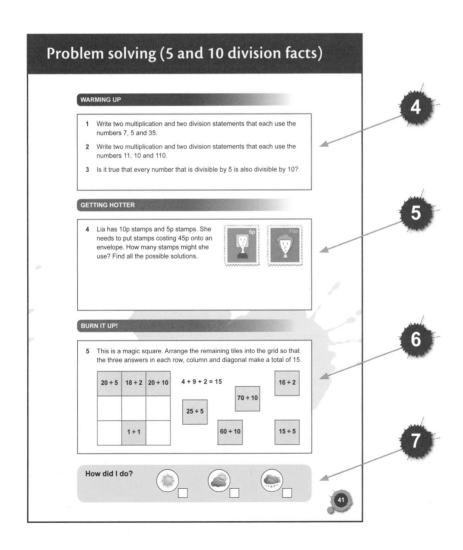

Multiplication table for 1

Look at the multiples of 1 above the line and the related multiplications below. Then cover them up and test yourself.

1	2	3	4	5	6	7	8	9	10	11	12

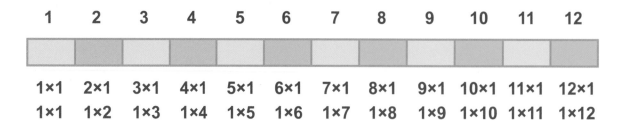

| 1×1 | 2×1 | 3×1 | 4×1 | 5×1 | 6×1 | 7×1 | 8×1 | 9×1 | 10×1 | 11×1 | 12×1 |
| 1×1 | 1×2 | 1×3 | 1×4 | 1×5 | 1×6 | 1×7 | 1×8 | 1×9 | 1×10 | 1×11 | 1×12 |

TEST 1

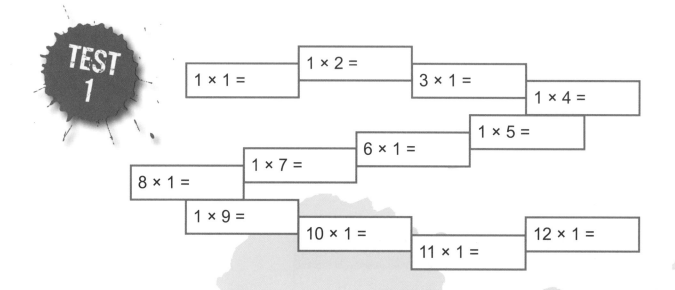

1 × 2 =

1 × 1 =

3 × 1 =

1 × 4 =

1 × 5 =

6 × 1 =

1 × 7 =

8 × 1 =

1 × 9 =

10 × 1 =

11 × 1 =

12 × 1 =

Remember too that zero times any number is zero, so 0 × 1 = 0, and 1 × 0 = 0.
Now test yourself again and time yourself.

TEST 2

1 × 11 =	8 × 1 =	1 × 4 =	7 × 1 =
3 × 1 =	1 × 10 =	9 × 1 =	1 × 0 =
1 × 12 =	1 × 1 =	0 × 1 =	1 × 2 =
10 × 1 =	5 × 1 =	1 × 6 =	11 × 1 =

Time taken:

Multiplication table for 1

Use your knowledge of the 1 times table to answer these questions.

1   How many £1 coins make up £7? ....
2   What are four ones? ....
3   What is one times seven? ....
4   Find the product of 3 and 1. ....
5   Multiply nine by one. ....
6   What is 12 multiplied by 1? ....
7   Zero times one equals what number? ....
8   What is one group of 11? ....
9   A cup of tea costs £1. How much for 8 cups? ....

10   Joe counts on in ones starting at 1. He says the multiples of 1 aloud.
     What is the 5th multiple of 1? ....

11   Chloe measures her stride. It is exactly 1 metre. She walks for 10 strides.
     How far is this in metres? ....

12   Mrs Jones is making jam. She buys three bags of sugar. Each weighs 1 kg.
     She also buys 2 kg of strawberries.
     How much does her shopping weigh? ....

Is each statement true or false?
13   Any whole number greater than zero is a multiple of 1. ....
14   If you multiply any number by 1, you always get the same number.

     ....

How did I do?

Division facts for 1

Look at the division facts below, cover them up, then test yourself.

0 ÷ 1 = 0	
1 ÷ 1 = 1	
2 ÷ 1 = 2	
3 ÷ 1 = 3	
4 ÷ 1 = 4	
5 ÷ 1 = 5	
6 ÷ 1 = 6	
7 ÷ 1 = 7	
8 ÷ 1 = 8	
9 ÷ 1 = 9	
10 ÷ 1 = 10	
11 ÷ 1 = 11	
12 ÷ 1 = 12	

TEST 1

0 ÷ 1 =

1 ÷ 1 =

2 ÷ 1 =

3 ÷ 1 =

4 ÷ 1 =

5 ÷ 1 =

6 ÷ 1 =

7 ÷ 1 =

8 ÷ 1 =

9 ÷ 1 =

10 ÷ 1 =

11 ÷ 1 =

12 ÷ 1 =

Write a sentence to explain what happens to a number when you divide it by 1.

....

These bags contain 1p coins. The totals of the coins are shown.
How many 1p coins are in each bag? Time yourself.

TEST 2

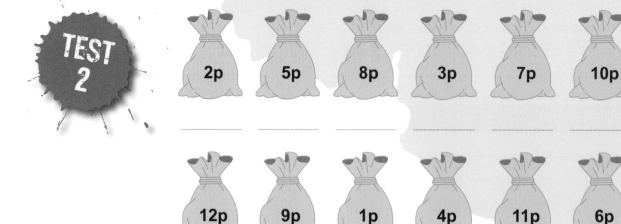

2p   5p   8p   3p   7p   10p

12p   9p   1p   4p   11p   6p

Time taken:

Division facts for 1

Use your knowledge of the division facts for the 1 times table to answer these questions.

1   How many £1 coins make up £7? ....

2   What is 5 divided by 1? ....

3   How many ones in 9? ....

4   Divide 12 by 1. ....

5   How many groups of 1 are in 1? ....

6   How many ones in ten? ....

7   What is zero divided by 1? ....

8   I need 8 kg of sugar. How many kilogram bags must I buy? ....

9   At a party, Kim makes a bowl of punch using 7 litres of orange juice. How many litre cartons of juice does she need? ....

10 In a car park, you must pay £1 for each hour of parking. For how many hours can you stay in the car park if you pay £3? ....

11 Garlic bulbs are sold in bags, with one bulb in each bag. How many bags would you buy if you needed 8 garlic bulbs? ....

Is each statement true or false?

12 When zero is divided by one the answer is one. ....

13 Dividing a number by 1 leaves the number unchanged. ....

How did I do?

Multiplication table for 2

Multiplying a number by 2 is the same as doubling, so 3 × 2 is double 3, and 12 × 2 is double 12.

Match the questions and answers with lines. Two have been done for you.

TEST 1

0 × 2
1 × 2
2 × 2
3 × 2
4 × 2
5 × 2
6 × 2
7 × 2
8 × 2
9 × 2
10 × 2
11 × 2
12 × 2

double 6
double 5
double 3
double 0
double 2
double 7
double 1
double 4
double 12
double 10
double 9
double 11
double 8

6
4
0
2
12
10
8
16
14
18
24
22
20

Now answer these questions as quickly as you can. Time yourself.

Remember, 2 × 6 has the same answer as 6 × 2, and so on.

TEST 2

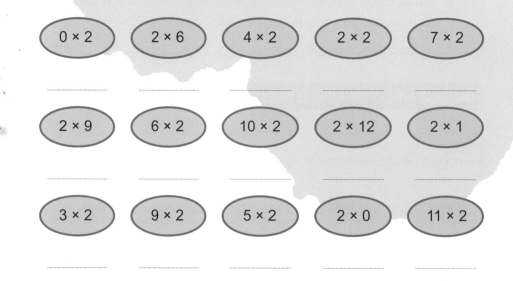

(0 × 2)   (2 × 6)   (4 × 2)   (2 × 2)   (7 × 2)

....

(2 × 9)   (6 × 2)   (10 × 2)   (2 × 12)   (2 × 1)

....

(3 × 2)   (9 × 2)   (5 × 2)   (2 × 0)   (11 × 2)

....

Time taken:

10

Multiplication table for 2

Remember that the answers to the 2 times table are even numbers.

WARMING UP

1   How much are six 2p coins worth? ....

2   What are two eights? ....

3   How many shoes in 7 pairs? ....

4   Multiply 12 by 2. ....

5   Find the product of 2 and 10. ....

6   How much are nine £2 coins? ....

7   What is double five? ....

8   What are eleven lots of two? ....

9   How many wheels on 8 bicycles? ....

GETTING HOTTER

10   When Sam was 8 years old, he got £6 pocket money each week.
       How much did Sam get in two weeks? ....

11   A shoot that was 4 cm tall last week has now doubled in size.
       How tall is it now? ....

12   There are two football teams playing each other. Each team has
       11 players. How many players is this altogether? ....

BURN IT UP!

13   A baby weighed 3 kg at birth. After 6 months, his weight had doubled.
       By the age of 2, his weight had doubled again. How much did he
       weigh at 2 years old? ....

14   Some apples are cut into halves. How many halves if there are
       12 apples? ....

How did I do?

 ☐   ☐   ☐

Division facts for 2

Dividing by 2 is the same as halving, so 6 ÷ 2 is half of 6, and 18 ÷ 2 is half of 18.

Match the questions and answers with lines. Two have been done for you.

TEST 1

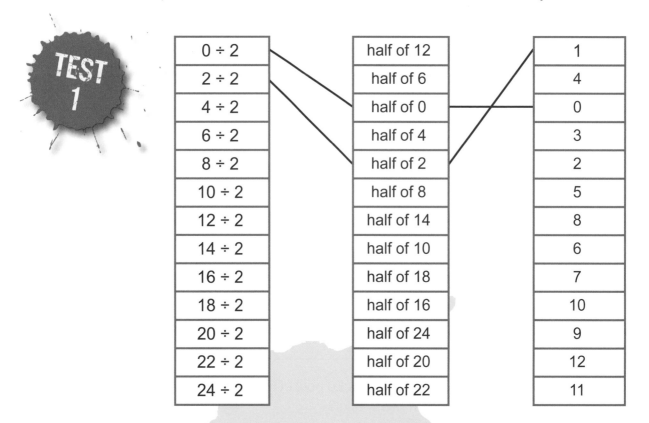

0 ÷ 2	half of 12	1
2 ÷ 2	half of 6	4
4 ÷ 2	half of 0	0
6 ÷ 2	half of 4	3
8 ÷ 2	half of 2	2
10 ÷ 2	half of 8	5
12 ÷ 2	half of 14	8
14 ÷ 2	half of 10	6
16 ÷ 2	half of 18	7
18 ÷ 2	half of 16	10
20 ÷ 2	half of 24	9
22 ÷ 2	half of 20	12
24 ÷ 2	half of 22	11

Now answer these questions as quickly as you can. Time yourself.

TEST 2

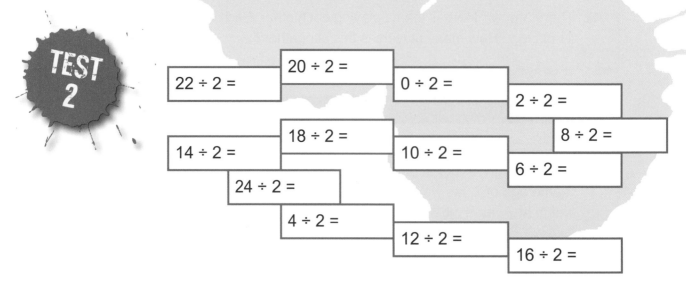

20 ÷ 2 =

22 ÷ 2 =

0 ÷ 2 =

2 ÷ 2 =

18 ÷ 2 =

8 ÷ 2 =

14 ÷ 2 =

10 ÷ 2 =

6 ÷ 2 =

24 ÷ 2 =

4 ÷ 2 =

12 ÷ 2 =

16 ÷ 2 =

Time taken:

Division facts for 2

Answer these questions using what you know about halving and dividing by 2.

WARMING UP

1. How many pairs can you make with 14 identical socks? ....
2. How many 2p coins make 20p? ....
3. Divide 16 by 2. ....
4. Share 12 sweets between two. ....
5. How many twos in twenty-four? ....
6. There are 18 people. They are put into two equal teams. How many in each team? ....
7. How many 2p sweets can you buy with 22p? ....

GETTING HOTTER

8. Onions come in packs of 2. How many packs should I buy if I need 14 onions altogether? ....

9. Tickets for a school play cost £2 each. How many tickets can Mrs Lee buy for £22? ....

BURN IT UP!

10. There were some sweets in a bowl. Chloe ate half of them. Then Samira ate half of the sweets that were left in the bowl, after Chloe had eaten hers. Six sweets were left in the bowl at the end. How many sweets were in the bowl at the start?

11. Divide each number by 2, using partitioning. One has been done for you.

26		32		38		36
20	6	30	2	30	8	
10	3					
	13					

How did I do?

 ☐   ☐   ☐

Look at the table below, cover it up, then test yourself.

1 × 5 = 5
2 × 5 = 10
3 × 5 = 15
4 × 5 = 20
5 × 5 = 25
6 × 5 = 30
7 × 5 = 35
8 × 5 = 40
9 × 5 = 45
10 × 5 = 50
11 × 5 = 55
12 × 5 = 60

TEST 1

1 × 5 =
2 × 5 =
3 × 5 =
4 × 5 =
5 × 5 =
6 × 5 =
7 × 5 =
8 × 5 =
9 × 5 =
10 × 5 =
11 × 5 =
12 × 5 =

Test yourself again and time how long it takes.

2 × 5 =
6 × 5 =
8 × 5 =
10 × 5 =
1 × 5 =
11 × 5 =
7 × 5 =
3 × 5 =
9 × 5 =
4 × 5 =
12 × 5 =
5 × 5 =

TEST 2

Don't forget that every multiple of 5 ends in 0 or 5.

An *odd* number multiplied by 5 ends in 5.

An *even* number multiplied by 5 ends in 0.

Time taken:

Multiplication table for 5

Try these questions about the 5 times table.

1   How much are nine 5p coins worth? _____

2   How many sides on 4 pentagons? _____

3   Find the product of 5 and 5. _____

4   How much are eight £5 notes worth? _____

5   What do five 10 g weights weigh? _____

6   Multiply 5 by 11. _____

7   What is five times zero? _____

8   How many toes on 7 feet? _____

9   How many in 12 groups of 5? _____

10   What are six fives? _____

GETTING HOTTER

11   Javed can walk at a speed of 5 kilometres per hour. How far can he walk in 4 hours? _____

12   Kieran is saving to buy an mp3 player costing £38. He has saved £5 each week for 7 weeks. How much more does he need to buy the mp3 player? _____

BURN IT UP!

13   How much will five chews cost, if two chews cost 24p? _____

14   Find the difference between 5 × 9 and 3 × 5. _____

15   Mr Day has a bottle that holds 100 ml of medicine. He takes 5 spoonfuls of medicine each day. The spoon holds 5 ml. For how many days will the medicine last? _____

How did I do?

 ☐   ☐   ☐

Division facts for 5

Division is the opposite of multiplication. 3 × 5 = 15 ⟶ 15 ÷ 5 = 3

Use 5 to write a division question for each multiplication question.

TEST 1

0 × 5 = 0   ⟶   0 ÷ 5 = 0   7 × 5 =   ⟶   ....

1 × 5 = 5   ⟶   5 ÷ 5 = 1   8 × 5 =   ⟶   ....

2 × 5 = 10   ⟶   10 ÷ 5 = ...   9 × 5 =   ⟶   ....

3 × 5 = 15   ⟶   ....   10 × 5 =   ⟶   ....

4 × 5 = 20   ⟶   ....   11 × 5 =   ⟶   ....

5 × 5 = 25   ⟶   ....   12 × 5 =   ⟶   ....

6 × 5 = 30   ⟶   ....

Now divide each of these numbers by 5 as quickly as you can. Time yourself.

TEST 2

| 10 | 35 | 55 | 20 |

| 5 | 45 | 50 | 15 | 30 |

| 40 | 25 | 60 | 0 |

Time taken:

16

Division facts for 5

Remember your division facts for the 5 times table to help you answer these questions.

WARMING UP

1   How many fives in 35? ....

2   Divide 15 by 5. ....

3   How many 5p coins make 45p? ....

4   60 players. How many teams of 5? ....

5   Share 20 between 5. ....

6   25 children are put into 5 teams. How many in each team? ....

7   How many 5 ml spoonfuls can be poured from 30 ml? ....

8   What is one-fifth of 50? ....

GETTING HOTTER

9   A snail crawled at a speed of 5 metres per hour without stopping. How long did it take him to crawl 40 metres? ....

10 The entrance fee to a funfair is £5. How many tickets can you buy with £55? ....

11 Carol is filling a paddling pool with 60 litres of water. How many 5-litre bucketfuls will she use to fill the pool? ....

BURN IT UP!

12 Divide 25 by 5 and then divide the answer by 5. What do you get? ....

13 If 5 biscuits cost 45p. How much would 2 biscuits cost? ....

14 What is the remainder when you divide 37 by 5? ....

How did I do?

 ☐   ☐   ☐

Multiplication table for 10

When a number is multiplied by 10, its digits move one column to the left.

H	T	U	
		7	× 10
7	0		

H	T	U	
	1	2	× 10
1	2	0	

Multiply each of these numbers by 10.

1	2	3	4	5	6
10					

7	8	9	10	11	12

Test yourself again and time how long it takes.

8 × 10 =		10 × 10 =		2 × 10 =
	7 × 10 =		3 × 10 =	
12 × 10 =		9 × 10 =		0 × 10 =
	6 × 10 =		5 × 10 =	
4 × 10 =		1 × 10 =		11 × 10 =

Time taken:

Multiplication table for 10

Use your knowledge of the 10 times table to answer these questions.

WARMING UP

1   How much are four 10p coins worth? ....

2   How many toes do 10 people have? ....

3   Find the product of 6 and 10. ....

4   10mm = 1cm. How many millimetres is the same as 4 cm? ....

5   Multiply 7 by 10. ....

6   Kim saves £10 each month. How much does she save in one year? ....

7   Jo has £10. Sam has five times as much. How much has Sam? ....

8   There are 11 players in each team. How many players in 10 teams? ....

GETTING HOTTER

9   In the school hall, 10 children can fit on each bench. How many children can fit on 7 benches? ....

10 Ben gave his four friends 10 stickers each and he had 7 left over. How many stickers did he have at first? ....

11 Mr Gregory finds a website that sells DVDs at £10 each. He buys 8 DVDs from the site and pays £92 for them including delivery. How much did he pay for delivery? ....

BURN IT UP!

12 How much greater than 4 × 10 is 10 × 11? ....

13 The Year 4 teacher at Milton School drives 10km to school each weekday and 10km home again. How far does she drive in total to and from work each week? ....

14 Is it true that multiplying by 5 is the same as multiplying by 10 and halving? ....

How did I do?

 ☐   ☐   ☐

Division facts for 10

When a number is divided by 10, its digits move one column to the right.

H	T	U	
	7	0	÷ 10
		7	

H	T	U	
1	2	0	÷ 10
	1	2	

Look at the division facts below, cover them up, then test yourself.

0 ÷ 10 = 0	
10 ÷ 10 = 1	
20 ÷ 10 = 2	
30 ÷ 10 = 3	
40 ÷ 10 = 4	
50 ÷ 10 = 5	
60 ÷ 10 = 6	
70 ÷ 10 = 7	
80 ÷ 10 = 8	
90 ÷ 10 = 9	
100 ÷ 10 = 10	
110 ÷ 10 = 11	
120 ÷ 10 = 12	

TEST 1

0 ÷ 10 =
10 ÷ 10 =
20 ÷ 10 =
30 ÷ 10 =
40 ÷ 10 =
50 ÷ 10 =
60 ÷ 10 =
70 ÷ 10 =
80 ÷ 10 =
90 ÷ 10 =
100 ÷ 10 =
110 ÷ 10 =
120 ÷ 10 =

Divide each number by 10. Time yourself.

TEST 2

110   90   100   70

10   20   80   60

70   50   120   30

Time taken:

Division facts for 10

Use the division facts for 10 to help you answer these questions.

WARMING UP

1   How many £10 notes make £90? ....

2   Divide 120 by 10. ....

3   Forty toes. How many people? ....

4   Share 30 sweets between 10. ....

5   How many 10 g weights make 60 g? ....

6   How many tens in 100? ....

7   10 mm = 1 cm. How many centimetres is the same as 40 mm? ....

8   A number multiplied by 10 is 110. What is the number? ....

GETTING HOTTER

9   At a netball tournament, 70 players get into 10 equal teams.
    How many players are there in each team? ....

10 How much change is left from £46 if Mick buys as many £10 pizzas as
    he can? ....

11 A decagon (a 10-sided polygon) has a perimeter of 80 cm. If all its
    sides are the same length, what is the length of each side? ....

BURN IT UP!

12 How many times larger is 120 ÷ 10 than 40 ÷ 10? ....

13 Jamal gives one-tenth of his money to charity each week. If he gets £100
    each week, how much does he give to charity in four weeks? ....

14 Ben's grandad is ten times older than Ben. If his grandad is 54 years older
    than Ben, can you work out how old Ben must be? ....

How did I do?

 ☐   ☐   ☐

21

Mixed multiplication practice (1 and 2)

The pink rods are 1 cube long and the green rods are 2 cubes long.
Write a multiplication fact for each row of rods. Two have been done for you.

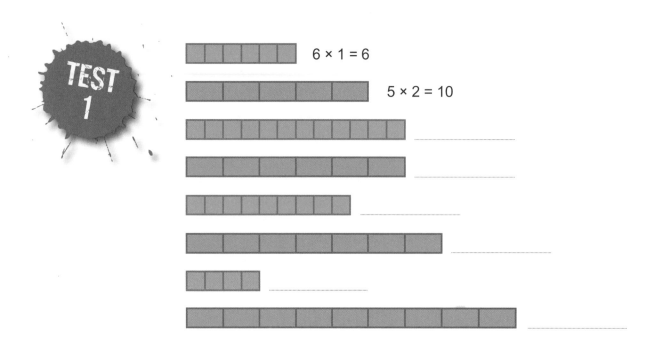

6 × 1 = 6

5 × 2 = 10

Complete these multiplications. Time yourself.

4 × 2 =	3 × 2 =	7 × 1 =
3 × 1 =	12 × 2 =	10 × 1 =
11 × 1 =	9 × 2 =	8 × 2 =
0 × 1 =	11 × 2 =	9 × 1 =
2 × 1 =	6 × 2 =	1 × 1 =

Time taken:

Mixed multiplication practice (1 and 2)

Use your knowledge of the 1 and 2 times tables to answer these questions.

WARMING UP

1   I have four 2p coins and three 1p coins. How much do I have? ....

2   What is the total of 7×1 and 5×2? ....

3   Find the difference between 10×2 and 9×1. ....

4   What is $2 \times 2 \times 2$? ....

5   How many £1 coins are worth the same as six £2 coins? ....

6   Ella has 8p. Kim has twice as much. How much do they have altogether?

....

7   Multiply zero by one. ....

8   What is $(5 \times 2) - (4 \times 1)$? ....

GETTING HOTTER

9   One half of a number is 12. What is the number? ....

10   There are seven teams of two players and one player left over.
How many players in total? ....

11   At a school fête, calendars are sold for £2 each and diaries for £1 each.
How much did the school get if it sold 12 calendars and 12 diaries?

....

BURN IT UP!

12   A hexagon has sides that are 1 cm long. A square has sides that are 2 cm
long. Which shape has the longer perimeter and by how much? ....

13   Answer each question:

     $1 \times 1 \times 1 \times 1$ $3 \times 2 \times 2 \times 2$ $7 \times 2 \times 7 \times 2 \times 0$

How did I do?

Mixed multiplication practice (5 and 10)

The blue rods are 5 cubes long and the orange rods are 10 cubes long. Write a multiplication fact for each row of rods. One has been done for you.

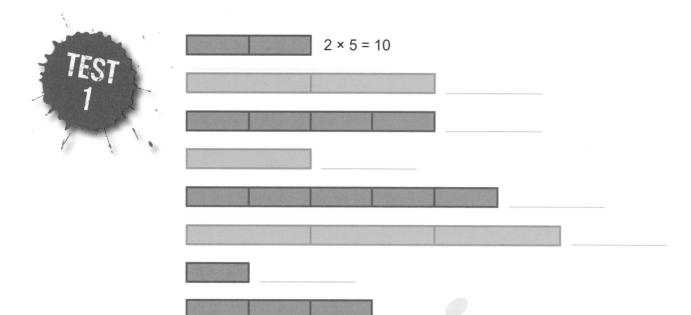

2 × 5 = 10

Answer these multiplications. Time yourself.

4 × 10 =	3 × 5 =	7 × 10 =
3 × 10 =	12 × 5 =	10 × 10 =
11 × 5 =	9 × 5 =	8 × 5 =
0 × 10 =	11 × 10 =	10 × 5 =
2 × 5 =	6 × 5 =	12 × 10 =

Time taken:

Mixed multiplication practice (5 and 10)

Use your knowledge of the 5 and 10 times tables to solve these problems.

WARMING UP

1   What is 2 × 5 × 10? ....

2   I have four 5p coins and three 10p coins. How much do I have? ....

3   Multiply five by ten by zero. What is the answer? ....

4   Find the difference between 4 × 10 and 7 × 5. ....

5   Add the product of 6 and 10 to the product of 2 and 5. ....

6   10 mm = 1 cm. How many millimetres is the same as 12 cm? ....

7   Add 6 × 5 and 9 × 10. ....

8   How many fives are the same as three tens? ....

GETTING HOTTER

9   Jonny and Donny have the same amount of money. Jonny has six £10 notes. If Donny only has £5 notes, how many does he have? ....

10 A shop sells T-shirts for £10 each and vest tops for £5 each. If it sells 7 T-shirts and 9 vest tops in one day, how much money did it get? ....

11 A box has 10 milk chocolates and 5 dark chocolates. How many chocolates are there altogether in 4 boxes? ....

BURN IT UP!

12 Subtract the number of days in one week from the number of days in ten weeks. ....

13 Are the answers to these the same? ....

   6 × 2 × 5 × 2   **10 × 3 × 2 × 2**

14 A bucket holds 5 litres of water. How many buckets of water would be needed to fill a pool that holds 600 litres? ....

How did I do?

 ☐   ☐   ☐

Mixed division practice (1 and 2)

The blue bags contain 1p coins. The orange bags contain 2p coins.
The totals of the coins are shown. How many coins in each bag?

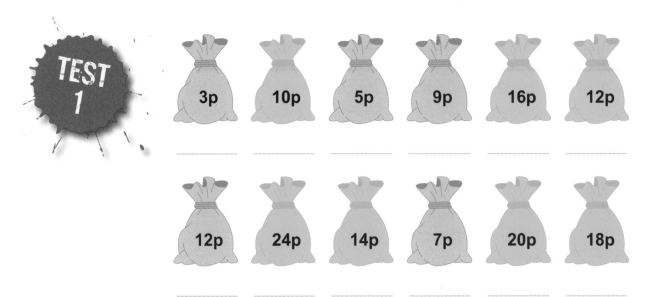

| 3p | 10p | 5p | 9p | 16p | 12p |

| 12p | 24p | 14p | 7p | 20p | 18p |

Answer these questions as quickly as you can. Time yourself.

TEST 2

8 ÷ 2 =	5 ÷ 1 =
1 ÷ 1 =	16 ÷ 2 =
6 ÷ 2 =	7 ÷ 1 =
4 ÷ 1 =	18 ÷ 2 =
12 ÷ 2 =	6 ÷ 1 =
12 ÷ 1 =	22 ÷ 2 =
10 ÷ 2 =	11 ÷ 1 =
0 ÷ 1 =	4 ÷ 2 =
20 ÷ 2 =	8 ÷ 1 =
2 ÷ 1 =	2 ÷ 2 =
24 ÷ 2 =	9 ÷ 1 =
3 ÷ 1 =	0 ÷ 2 =
14 ÷ 2 =	10 ÷ 1 =

Time taken:

Mixed division practice (1 and 2)

Use your knowledge of the division facts from the 1 and 2 times tables to help you solve these.

WARMING UP

1   How many £2 coins make £18? ....

2   Divide 12 by 2 and divide the answer by 1. What do you get? ....

3   How many twos are the same as 12 ones? ....

4   How many ones are the same as 5 twos? ....

5   How many groups of two can be made from 15? ....

6   Find the difference between 24 ÷ 2 and 5 ÷ 1. ....

7   What is the remainder when 23 is divided by 2? ....

8   What is zero divided by one? ....

GETTING HOTTER

9   Some peaches are cut in half. If there are 22 halves, how many whole peaches were there? ....

10   A shop sells 1 kg bags of potatoes for £2 each. Claire pays £18 for some bags of potatoes. How many kilograms of potatoes did she buy? ....

11   In a car park, you must pay £2 for each hour of parking. For how many hours can you stay in the car park if you pay £8? ....

BURN IT UP!

12   If eight cups of coffee cost £16, how much do three cups of coffee cost?

....

13   Squaring a number means multiplying it by itself. What number squared gives the answer 4? ....

14   True or false: dividing a number by 1 always gives the answer 1?

....

How did I do?

Mixed division practice (5 and 10)

Finding one-fifth, $\frac{1}{5}$, is the same as dividing by 5. Finding one-tenth, $\frac{1}{10}$, is the same as dividing by 10. Write the value of each:

One-fifth of 45 ⎯⎯⎯⎯⎯⎯⎯⎯⎯ One-tenth of 110 ⎯⎯⎯⎯⎯⎯⎯

$\frac{1}{5}$ of 10 ⎯⎯⎯⎯⎯⎯⎯⎯⎯⎯⎯⎯⎯ $\frac{1}{10}$ of 60 ⎯⎯⎯⎯⎯⎯⎯⎯⎯⎯⎯⎯

One-fifth of 30 ⎯⎯⎯⎯⎯⎯⎯⎯⎯ $\frac{1}{10}$ of 20 ⎯⎯⎯⎯⎯⎯⎯⎯⎯⎯⎯⎯

One-tenth of 90 ⎯⎯⎯⎯⎯⎯⎯⎯⎯ $\frac{1}{5}$ of 25 ⎯⎯⎯⎯⎯⎯⎯⎯⎯⎯⎯⎯

$\frac{1}{5}$ of 55 ⎯⎯⎯⎯⎯⎯⎯⎯⎯⎯⎯⎯⎯ One-tenth of 100 ⎯⎯⎯⎯⎯⎯⎯

One-fifth of 35 ⎯⎯⎯⎯⎯⎯⎯⎯⎯ $\frac{1}{10}$ of 10 ⎯⎯⎯⎯⎯⎯⎯⎯⎯⎯⎯⎯

$\frac{1}{5}$ of 40 ⎯⎯⎯⎯⎯⎯⎯⎯⎯⎯⎯⎯⎯ One-fifth of 60 ⎯⎯⎯⎯⎯⎯⎯⎯⎯

One-tenth of 120 ⎯⎯⎯⎯⎯⎯⎯⎯

Answer these questions as quickly as you can. Time yourself.

40 ÷ 5 =	100 ÷ 10 =
40 ÷ 10 =	35 ÷ 5 =
25 ÷ 5 =	90 ÷ 10 =
30 ÷ 10 =	30 ÷ 5 =
5 ÷ 5 =	120 ÷ 10 =
80 ÷ 10 =	0 ÷ 5 =
10 ÷ 5 =	60 ÷ 10 =
110 ÷ 10 =	15 ÷ 5 =
55 ÷ 5 =	70 ÷ 10 =
10 ÷ 10 =	60 ÷ 5 =
20 ÷ 5 =	0 ÷ 10 =
20 ÷ 10 =	45 ÷ 5 =
50 ÷ 5 =	50 ÷ 10 =

Time taken:

Mixed division practice (5 and 10)

Can you solve these problems using the division facts you know?

WARMING UP

1. 10 mm = 1 cm. How many centimetres is the same as 110 mm? _____
2. Add (100 ÷ 10) to (10 ÷ 5). _____
3. How many less than one-fifth of 40 is one-tenth of 50? _____
4. How much less than 58p are eight 5p coins worth? _____
5. How many £5 notes make £55? _____
6. How many £10 notes make £120? _____
7. Share 50 between 10 and divide the answer by 5. _____
   What do you get? _____
8. What is the remainder when 99 is divided by 10? _____

GETTING HOTTER

9. Zofia has 90p made from 5p and 10p coins. If she has five 10p coins, how many 5p coins does she have? _____

10. At a theme park, each person must pay a £10 entrance fee and then each ride costs £5. Amy and her mum spent a total of £75. They both paid the entrance fee. How many rides did they pay for? _____

BURN IT UP!

11. The equals sign shows that what is on one side is equal to what is on the other side. For example: 2 × 5 = 1 × 10 ; 100 ÷ 10 = 2 × 5.

    Fill in the missing numbers so that each statement is true.

    20 ÷ [   ] = 40 ÷ 10   [   ] ÷ 10 = 55 ÷ 5

    [   ] ÷ 10 = 40 ÷ 5   10 ÷ [   ] = 5 ÷ 5

    20 ÷ 10 = [   ] ÷ 5   120 ÷ 10 = [   ] ÷ 5

How did I do?

 ☐   ☐   ☐

Each pile of coins contains 1p, 2p, 5p or 10p coins. How much money is in each pile?

TEST 1

4 × 1p

5 × 2p

6 × 5p

7 × 10p

12 × 5p

8 × 1p

6 × 10p

9 × 2p

4 × 10p

8 × 2p

3 × 1p

11 × 5p

Multiply the number at the left of each row by the number at the top of each column to complete the table. Time yourself.

TEST 2

×	3	7	9	12
1	3			
2			18	
5				
10		70		

Time taken:

30

Mixed multiplication practice (1, 2, 5 and 10)

Use your knowledge of these times tables to answer these questions.

WARMING UP

1 How many twos are equal to four fives? ....

2 Find the product of 6 and 10. ....

3 Find 3 × 2 and multiply the answer by 5. ....

4 Find the difference between 2 × 12 and 3 × 5. ....

5 Subtract 8 × 2 from 4 × 5. ....

6 Find the total of six 5p coins, three 2p coins and four 10p coins. ....

7 Add 7 × 5, 6 × 2 and 3 × 1. ....

8 What are 3 groups of 10 plus 4 groups of 2? ....

9 How much does it cost to buy eight 5p sweets and two 10p sweets?

    ....

GETTING HOTTER

10 Billy and Milly have the same amount of money. Billy has twelve £5 notes and five £2 coins. Milly only has £10 notes; how many does she have?

    ....

11 A set of balance scales has eight 10 g weights in one pan. How many 5 g weights need to be put in the other pan for the scale to balance?

    ....

BURN IT UP!

12 Sam has some 2p coins, some 5p coins and some 10p coins. He has a total of 97p. If he has six 2p coins and three 5p coins, how many 10p coins has he? ....

13 I'm thinking of a secret number. I multiply it by 10. I also multiply it by 5. When I add the two answers I get 165. What is my secret number?

    ....

How did I do?

31

Mixed division practice (1, 2, 5 and 10)

For each number of players, use division to show how many different-sized teams there would be.

10 players

in teams of 10

in teams of 5

in teams of 2

40 players

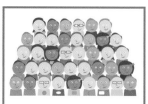

in teams of 10

in teams of 5

in teams of 2

20 players

in teams of 10

in teams of 5

in teams of 2

30 players

in teams of 10

in teams of 5

in teams of 2

Now write how many would be left out if the children got into these different teams. Time yourself.

21 players

in teams of 10

in teams of 5

in teams of 2

36 players

in teams of 10

in teams of 5

in teams of 2

17 players

in teams of 10

in teams of 5

in teams of 2

33 players

in teams of 10

in teams of 5

in teams of 2

Time taken:

32

Mixed division practice (1, 2, 5 and 10)

Use division facts to help you solve these questions.

WARMING UP

1   Divide 40 by 5 and the answer by 2. What number do you get? ....
2   How many groups of 5 in 55? ....
3   One-fifth of 35 is half of what number? ....
4   Add one-tenth of 120 to one half of 24. ....
5   Add $(90 \div 10)$ to $(16 \div 2)$. ....
6   How many £2 coins make the same as two £5 notes? ....
7   Find $\frac{1}{2}$ of 18 and multiply the answer by 5. ....
8   Find the difference between $40 \div 5$ and $5 \div 1$. ....
9   What is zero divided by five? ....

GETTING HOTTER

10 When 30 is divided by 5 you get the same answer as a number divided by 2. What is that number? ....

11 Lia's father is 5 times older than she is. Her grandma is 10 times older than she is. If Lia's grandma is 70, how old is Lia's father? ....

12 Each of the 10 pods of a Ferris wheel can hold 10 people. There are 68 people on the wheel, and 6 pods are full. The other 4 pods have an equal number of people in them. How many people are in each of these 4 pods? ....

BURN IT UP!

13 I'm thinking of a secret number. When it is divided by 5, the remainder is 2. When it is divided by 10, the remainder is 7. What is the remainder when it is divided by 2? ....

14 A water slide takes a photo of you getting soaked on the way down! Over 2 hours, 6 people each hour buy a photo, spending a total of £120. How much does a photo cost? ....

How did I do?

33

Problem solving (1 and 2 times tables)

Fill in the missing numbers in these multiplications. Time yourself.

4 × 2 = [   ]   [   ] × 1 = 6   5 × [   ] = 10

1 × [   ] = 1   4 × [   ] = 4   [   ] × 2 = 0

1 × 6 = [   ]   [   ] × 6 = 12   2 × [   ] = 18

[   ] × 2 = 4   8 × 2 = [   ]   [   ] × 1 = 12

2 × [   ] = 14   7 × [   ] = 7   11 × 2 = [   ]

This is a magic square. The three numbers in each row, column and diagonal add up to 15. Multiply each number in the square by 2 to create a new set of numbers. Time yourself.

6	7	2
1	5	9
8	3	4

12		

Is the new square a magic square? If so, what do the numbers add up to? ....

Time taken: [   ]

Problem solving (1 and 2 times tables)

Use your knowledge of these times tables to answer these questions.

WARMING UP

1 Add the sixth multiple of 2 to the ninth multiple of 1. ....

2 Is it true that every multiple of 2 is also a multiple of 1? ....

3 Write 6 pairs of tables facts for the 1 and 2 times tables that have the same answers. ....

GETTING HOTTER

4 Use these digit cards to make as many different tables facts as you can. You can use each card as many times as you like, for example: 1 × 1 = 1, 11 × 2 = 22. Can you make at least 6 different facts from the 1 times table and at least 6 from the 2 times table?

| 0 | 1 | 2 | 3 | 4 | × | = |

BURN IT UP!

5 Kim has £9 in £1 and £2 coins in her purse. How many coins might she have? Is it possible that she has 4 coins, 5 coins, 6 coins, 7 coins or 8 coins? Find all the different combinations of coins she could have.

6 Jo has written some facts from a times table, but has used letters to stand for digits. Is this the one times table or the two times table?

A × ? = A   F × ? = F   G × ? = G   C × ? = C
H × ? = H   B × ? = B   D × ? = D   E × ? = E

Explain your answer in words. ....

How did I do?

 ☐   ☐   ☐

Problem solving (1 and 2 division facts)

Write a division fact for the 2 times table that gives each number on the clock.

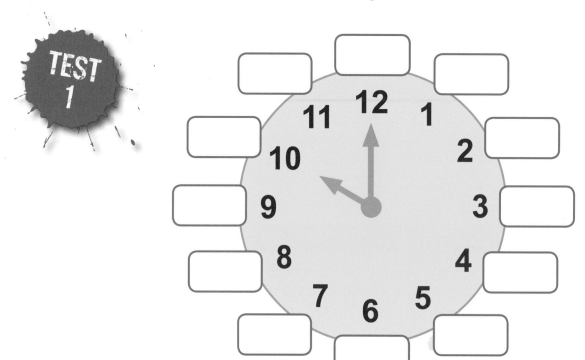

Fill in the missing numbers in these divisions. Time yourself.

4 ÷ 2 = [   ]   [   ] ÷ 1 = 9   20 ÷ [   ] = 10

[   ] ÷ 1 = 1   14 ÷ [   ] = 7   [   ] ÷ 2 = 0

6 ÷ 1 = [   ]   [   ] ÷ 2 = 9   2 ÷ [   ] = 1

[   ] ÷ 2 = 4   8 ÷ 2 = [   ]   [   ] ÷ 1 = 12

22 ÷ [   ] = 11   7 ÷ [   ] = 7   [   ] ÷ 2 = 12

Time taken:

Problem solving (1 and 2 division facts)

1   Write a word problem for each of these questions:

$4 \div 1 = ?$

$0 \div 2 = ?$

$24 \div 2 = ?$

2   Use these digit cards to make as many different division facts as you can. You can use each card as many times as you like, for example: $1 \div 1 = 1$, $12 \div 0 = 0$. Can you make more than 10 different division facts from the 1 and 2 times tables?

| 0 | 1 | 2 | 3 | 4 | ÷ | = |

....

....

....

3   This is a magic square. Arrange the remaining tiles into the grid so that the three answers in each row, column and diagonal add up to 15.

$16 \div 2$	$2 \div 2$	$12 \div 2$
		$14 \div 2$
	$18 \div 2$	

$8 + 1 + 6 = 15$

$8 \div 2$

$4 \div 2$ $6 \div 2$ $10 \div 2$

How did I do?

37

Problem solving (5 and 10 times tables)

Fill in the missing numbers in these multiplications. Time yourself.

11 × 10 = [   ]   [   ] × 5 = 30   5 × [   ] = 25

10 × [   ] = 100   4 × [   ] = 20   [   ] × 10 = 0

1 × 5 = [   ]   [   ] × 5 = 35   5 × [   ] = 40

[   ] × 10 = 10   9 × 5 = [   ]   [   ] × 10 = 40

9 × [   ] = 90   5 × [   ] = 15   5 × 10 = [   ]

This is a magic square. The three numbers in each row, column and diagonal add up to 15. Multiply each number in the square by 5 to create a new set of numbers. Time yourself.

4	9	2
3	5	7
8	1	6

20		

Is the new square a magic square? If so, what do the numbers add up to? ....

Time taken:

Problem solving (5 and 10 times tables)

WARMING UP

1 Add the eighth multiple of 5 to the fifth multiple of 10. ....

2 Write 6 pairs of tables facts for the 5 and 10 times tables that have the same answers.

GETTING HOTTER

3 Follow these rules for numbers between 1 and 12.

> **If it is even, multiply by 5, then divide the answer by 10.**
> **If it is odd, multiply by 5, then add 5 and divide by 10.**

Write what each number from 1 to 12 becomes if the rules are followed.

4 Use the clues to complete this puzzle. Write multiplications for the missing clues.

	Across	
1 7 × 5		**6** 3 × 5
2 4 × 5		**7** 8 × 5
3 9 × 5		**8** 9 × 10
4 5 × 10		

	Down	
1 3 × 10		**5** 6 × 10
2 5 × 5		**6** 2 × 5
3 ...... ×		**7** 4 × 10
4 ...... ×		

BURN IT UP!

5 Jo has written some facts from a times table, but has used letters to stand for digits. Is this the ten times table or the five times table?

A × ? = AC   F × ? = FC   C × ? = C   B × ? = BC
H × ? = HC   G × ? = GC   D × ? = DC   E × ? = EC

Explain your answer in words. ....

....

How did I do?

 ☐   ☐   ☐

Problem solving (5 and 10 division facts)

Write a division fact for the 5 times table that gives each number on the clock.

Fill in the missing numbers in these divisions. Time yourself.

40 ÷ 5 = [   ]   [   ] ÷ 10 = 9   50 ÷ [   ] = 10

5 ÷ [   ] = 1   35 ÷ [   ] = 7   [   ] ÷ 5 = 0

10 ÷ 5 = [   ]   [   ] ÷ 5 = 9   10 ÷ [   ] = 1

[   ] ÷ 5 = 4   30 ÷ 5 = [   ]   [   ] ÷ 10 = 12

55 ÷ [   ] = 11   70 ÷ [   ] = 7   [   ] ÷ 5 = 12

Time taken:

40

Problem solving (5 and 10 division facts)

1   Write two multiplication and two division statements that each use the numbers 7, 5 and 35.

2   Write two multiplication and two division statements that each use the numbers 11, 10 and 110.

3   Is it true that every number that is divisible by 5 is also divisible by 10?

4   Lia has 10p stamps and 5p stamps. She needs to put stamps costing 45p onto an envelope. How many stamps might she use? Find all the possible solutions.

5   This is a magic square. Arrange the remaining tiles into the grid so that the three answers in each row, column and diagonal make a total of 15.

20 ÷ 5	18 ÷ 2	20 ÷ 10
	1 ÷ 1	

4 + 9 + 2 = 15

25 ÷ 5

70 ÷ 10

16 ÷ 2

60 ÷ 10

15 ÷ 5

How did I do?

Problem solving (1, 2, 5 and 10 times tables)

Fill in the missing numbers so that every joined question has the same answer.

TEST 1

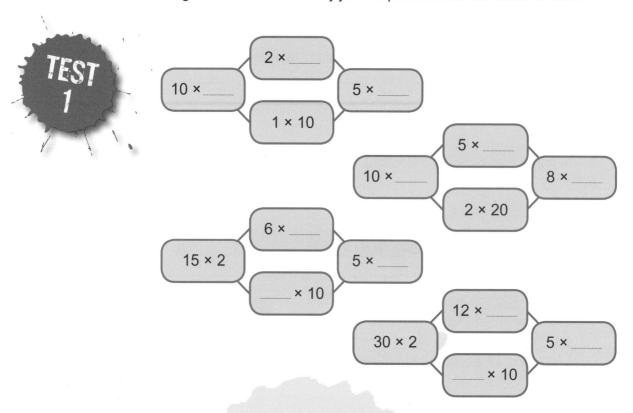

2 × _____

10 × _____

5 × _____

1 × 10

5 × _____

10 × _____

8 × _____

2 × 20

6 × _____

15 × 2

5 × _____

_____ × 10

12 × _____

30 × 2

5 × _____

_____ × 10

Fill in the missing numbers in these divisions. Time yourself.

TEST 2

11 × 1 = [ ]	[ ] × 2 = 24	5 × [ ] = 25
10 × [ ] = 120	4 × [ ] = 20	[ ] × 1 = 0
7 × 2 = [ ]	[ ] × 5 = 35	4 × [ ] = 40
[ ] × 10 = 10	9 × 2 = [ ]	[ ] × 1 = 4
8 × [ ] = 80	5 × [ ] = 45	12 × 5 = [ ]

Time taken:

Problem solving (1, 2, 5 and 10 times tables)

1   Answer these questions:

    $5 \times 2 \times 5 =$ _____ $4 \times 5 \times 0 =$ _____ $1 \times 1 \times 5 \times 5 =$ _____ $7 \times 5 \times 8 \times 0 =$ _____

2   What is the ninth multiple of 2 plus the seventh multiple of 1? _____

3   The answer is 20. What could the question be?

GETTING HOTTER

4   Fill in the missing digits to make each answer correct.

    Can you complete the second grid in the same way?

    Make up more of your own puzzles.

	3 × 5	4 × 5
6 × 2	**1**	**2**
5 × 10		

	↓	↓
7 × 2		
11 × 5		

BURN IT UP!

5   Use these digit cards to make as many different tables facts as you can. You can use each card as many times as you like, for example: $0 \times 10 = 0$, $2 \times 5 = 10$. Can you make more than 20 different facts from your 1, 2, 5 and 10 times tables?

| 0 | 1 | 2 | 3 | 4 | 5 | × | = |

How did I do?

 ☐   ☐   ☐

Problem solving (1, 2, 5 and 10 division facts)

Find sets of questions with the same answer. Colour each set the same colour.

TEST 1

90 ÷ 10	0 ÷ 10	50 ÷ 10	40 ÷ 5	14 ÷ 2
35 ÷ 5	12 ÷ 2	30 ÷ 5	20 ÷ 2	100 ÷ 10
45 ÷ 5	25 ÷ 5	18 ÷ 2	5 ÷ 5	0 ÷ 2
20 ÷ 10	3 ÷ 1	30 ÷ 10	1 ÷ 1	80 ÷ 10
15 ÷ 5	60 ÷ 10	16 ÷ 2	10 ÷ 5	50 ÷ 5
4 ÷ 2	40 ÷ 10	20 ÷ 5	8 ÷ 2	70 ÷ 10

Fill in the missing numbers in these divisions. Time yourself.

TEST 2

22 ÷ 2 = [   ]   [   ] ÷ 10 = 7   20 ÷ [   ] = 10

45 ÷ 5 = [   ]   [   ] ÷ 2 = 8   [   ] ÷ 1 = 0

[   ] ÷ 5 = 8   110 ÷ 10 = [   ]   [   ] ÷ 5 = 12

18 ÷ [   ] = 9   120 ÷ [   ] = 12   [   ] ÷ 2 = 12

Time taken:

Problem solving (1, 2, 5 and 10 division facts)

1   Kim spent £1 on 10p, 2p and 5p stamps. She bought twice as many 5p stamps as 2p stamps. If she bought four 10p stamps, which other stamps did she buy? ....

2   Find the total of the ninth multiple of 2, the fourth multiple of 5, the second multiple of 1 and the seventh multiple of 10.

....

....

GETTING HOTTER

3   Use these digit cards to make as many different division facts as you can. You can use each card as many times as you like, for example: 5 ÷ 1 = 5, 10 ÷ 2 = 5. Can you make more than 20 different division facts related to the 1, 2, 5 and 10 times tables?

| 0 | 1 | 2 | 3 | 4 | 5 | ÷ | = |

BURN IT UP!

4   Use the clues to fill in this puzzle. Write divisions or multiplications for the missing clues.

Across
1   24 ÷ 2
2   2 × 7
3   11 × 2
4   3 × 5

6   ....
7   ....
8   30 ÷ 2

Down
1   110 ÷ 10
2   60 ÷ 5
3   5 × 5
4   100 ÷ 10

5   4 × 10
6   11 × 5
7   7 × 5

How did I do?

 □   □   □

Hints and tips

When learning your times tables and related division facts there are some useful things to remember:

- The order of the numbers in a multiplication question doesn't matter as the answer will be the same, for example 6 × 2 = 12 and 2 × 6 = 12. It means that you learn two facts for the price of one!

- If you know multiplication facts then you also know related division facts. If you know that 6 × 2 = 12 and 2 × 6 = 12 then you also know that 12 ÷ 2 = 6 and 12 ÷ 6 = 2. This means that you actually learn four facts for the price of one!

- You might find it easier to learn the facts in order at first, but make sure that you begin to learn to answer questions in any order.

- Look for patterns in the numbers to help you check your answers. For example: the answers for the facts in the 2, 4, 6 and 8 times tables are always even; the answers to the 10 times table end in 0; the answers to the 5 times table end in 0 or 5; the digits of the answers to the 9 times table always add up to 9 or 18 and so on.

- As you learn a table there will always be some facts that you find more difficult to remember than others. Focus on learning these facts using the tips below.

Try these different approaches:

- Say facts aloud using a range of voices: high or low voices, whispering, croaking, singing, shouting, speaking with the voice of a cat, snake, worm, monster and so on.

- Write questions onto small pieces of paper or card and the answers on the other side. Use them to test yourself at different times. Put them on the fridge, on a noticeboard or even on your stairs. Each time you see the card try to remember the answer.

- Draw pictures for the questions you find most difficult, such as drawing a picture of 5 rows of 9 flowers to help you with the question 'How many 5s in 45?'

- Write out facts in words rather than just using numbers, such as for 24 ÷ 2 writing 'twenty-four divided by two is twelve'.

- Make up rhymes and songs to help you learn facts that you find difficult to remember, such as 'Clap, bang, thump the floor because 8 times 8 is sixty-four' or 'Turn off the telly and touch the screen as 4 lots of 4 equals sixteen'. Use movements and gestures in the rhymes as this can also help you to remember them more easily.

Answers

Multiplication table for 1 (pages 6–7)

Test 1 1, 2, 3, 4, 5, 6, 7, 8, 9, 10, 11, 12

Test 2 11, 8, 4, 7
3, 10, 9, 0
12, 1, 0, 2
10, 5, 6, 11

1 7	**2** 4	**3** 7
4 3	**5** 9	**6** 12
7 0	**8** 11	**9** £8
10 5	**11** 10 m	**12** 5 kg
13 True	**14** True	

Division facts for 1 (pages 8–9)

Test 1 0, 1, 2, 3, 4, 5, 6, 7, 8, 9, 10, 11, 12
The number doesn't change.

Test 2 2, 5, 8, 3, 7, 10
12, 9, 1, 4, 11, 6

1 7	**2** 5	**3** 9
4 12	**5** 1	**6** 10
7 0	**8** 8	**9** 7
10 3 hours	**11** 8	
12 False – the answer is zero.		**13** True

Multiplication table for 2 (pages 10–11)

Test 1

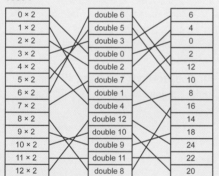

0 × 2	double 6	6
1 × 2	double 5	4
2 × 2	double 3	0
3 × 2	double 0	2
4 × 2	double 2	12
5 × 2	double 7	10
6 × 2	double 1	8
7 × 2	double 4	16
8 × 2	double 12	14
9 × 2	double 10	18
10 × 2	double 9	24
11 × 2	double 11	22
12 × 2	double 8	20

Test 2 0, 12, 8, 4, 14
18, 12, 20, 24, 2
6, 18, 10, 0, 22

1 12p	**2** 16	**3** 14
4 24	**5** 20	**6** £18
7 10	**8** 22	**9** 16
10 £12	**11** 8 cm	**12** 22
13 12 kg	**14** 24	

Division facts for 2 (pages 12–13)

Test 1

0 ÷ 2	half of 12	1
2 ÷ 2	half of 6	4
4 ÷ 2	half of 0	0
6 ÷ 2	half of 4	3
8 ÷ 2	half of 2	2
10 ÷ 2	half of 8	5
12 ÷ 2	half of 14	8
14 ÷ 2	half of 10	6
16 ÷ 2	half of 18	7
18 ÷ 2	half of 16	10
20 ÷ 2	half of 24	9
22 ÷ 2	half of 20	12
24 ÷ 2	half of 22	11

Test 2 11, 10, 0, 1, 4, 3, 5, 9, 7, 12, 2, 6, 8

1 7	**2** 10	**3** 8
4 6	**5** 12	**6** 9
7 11	**8** 7	**9** 11
10 24	**11** 16, 19, 18	

Multiplication table for 5 (pages 14–15)

Test 1 5, 10, 15, 20, 25, 30, 35, 40, 45, 50, 55, 60

Test 2 10, 30, 40, 50, 5, 55, 35, 15, 45, 20, 60, 25

1 45p	**2** 20	**3** 25
4 £40	**5** 50 g	**6** 55
7 0	**8** 35	**9** 60
10 30	**11** 20 km	**12** £3
13 60p	**14** 30	**15** 4 days

Division facts for 5 (pages 16–17)

Test 1

$0 \div 5 = 0,$	$5 \div 5 = 1,$	$10 \div 5 = 2,$
$15 \div 5 = 3,$	$20 \div 5 = 4,$	$25 \div 5 = 5,$
$30 \div 5 = 6,$	$35 \div 5 = 7,$	$40 \div 5 = 8,$
$45 \div 5 = 9,$	$50 \div 5 = 10,$	$55 \div 5 = 11,$
$60 \div 5 = 12$		

Test 2 2, 7, 11, 4
1, 9, 10, 3, 6
8, 5, 12, 0

1 7	**2** 3	**3** 9
4 12	**5** 4	**6** 5
7 6	**8** 10	**9** 8 hours
10 11	**11** 12	**12** 1
13 18p	**14** 2	

Multiplication table for 10 (pages 18–19)

Test 1 10, 20, 30, 40, 50, 60, 70, 80, 90, 100, 110, 120

Test 2 80, 100, 20
70, 30
120, 90, 0
60, 50
40, 10, 110

1 40p	**2** 100	**3** 60
4 40	**5** 70	**6** £120
7 £50	**8** 110	**9** 70
10 47	**11** £12	**12** 70
13 100 km	**14** Yes	

Division facts for 10 (pages 20–21)

Test 1 0, 1, 2, 3, 4, 5, 6, 7, 8, 9, 10, 11, 12

Test 2 11, 9, 10, 7
1, 2, 8, 6
7, 5, 12, 3

1 9	**2** 12	**3** 4
4 3	**5** 6	**6** 10
7 4	**8** 11	**9** 7
10 £6	**11** 8 cm	**12** 3
13 £40	**14** 6	

Mixed multiplication practice (1 and 2) (pages 22–23)

Test 1 $12 \times 1 = 12,$ $6 \times 2 = 12,$ $9 \times 1 = 9,$
$7 \times 2 = 14,$ $4 \times 1 = 4,$ $9 \times 2 = 18$

Test 2 8, 6, 7
3, 24, 10
11, 18, 16
0, 22, 9
2, 12, 1

1 11p	**2** 17	**3** 11
4 8	**5** 12	**6** 24p
7 0	**8** 6	**9** 24
10 15	**11** £36	

12 The perimeter of the square is 2 cm longer.
13 1, 24, 0

Mixed multiplication practice (5 and 10) (pages 24–25)

Test 1 $2 \times 10 = 20,$ $4 \times 5 = 20,$ $1 \times 10 = 10,$
$5 \times 5 = 25,$ $3 \times 10 = 30,$ $1 \times 5 = 5,$
$3 \times 5 = 15,$ $6 \times 5 = 30$

Test 2 40, 15, 70
30, 60, 100
55, 45, 40
0, 110, 50
10, 30, 120

1 100	**2** 50p	**3** 0
4 5	**5** 70	**6** 120
7 120	**8** 6	**9** 12
10 £115	**11** 60	**12** 63
13 Yes	**14** 120	

Mixed division practice (1 and 2) (pages 26–27)

Test 1 3, 5, 5, 9, 8, 6
12, 12, 7, 7, 10, 9

Test 2 4, 1, 3, 4, 6, 12, 5, 0, 10, 2, 12, 3, 7
5, 8, 7, 9, 6, 11, 11, 2, 8, 1, 9, 0, 10

1 9	**2** 6	**3** 6
4 10	**5** 7	**6** 7
7 1	**8** 0	**9** 11
10 9	**11** 4	**12** £6
13 2	**14** False	

Mixed division practice (5 and 10) (pages 28–29)

Test 1 9   11
2   6
6   2
9   5
11   10
7   1
8   12
12

Test 2 8, 4, 5, 3, 1, 8, 2, 11, 11, 1, 4, 2, 10
10, 7, 9, 6, 12, 0, 6, 3, 7, 12, 0, 9, 5

1 11	**2** 12	**3** 3
4 18p	**5** 11	**6** 12
7 1	**8** 9	**9** 8
10 11	**11** 5, 110 80, 10 10, 60	

Mixed multiplication practice (1, 2, 5 and 10) (pages 30–31)

Test 1 4p, 10p, 30p, 70p
60p, 8p, 60p, 18p
40p, 16p, 3p, 55p

Answers

Test 2 3, 7, 9, 12
6, 14, 18, 24
15, 35, 45, 60
30, 70, 90, 120

1	10	**2**	60	**3**	30
4	9	**5**	4	**6**	76p
7	50	**8**	38	**9**	60p
10	7	**11**	16	**12**	7
13	11				

Mixed division practice (1, 2, 5 and 10) (pages 32–33)

Test 1 1, 2, 5   4, 8, 20
2, 4, 10   3, 6, 15

Test 2 1, 1, 1   6, 1, 0
7, 2, 1   3, 3, 1

1	4	**2**	11	**3**	14
4	24	**5**	17	**6**	5
7	45	**8**	3	**9**	0
10	12	**11**	35	**12**	2
13	1	**14**	£10		

Problem solving (1 and 2 times tables) (pages 34–35)

Test 1 8, 6, 2
1, 1, 0
6, 2, 9
2, 16, 12
7, 1, 22

Test 2 12, 14, 4
2, 10, 18
16, 6, 8
Yes, totals add up to 30

1 21

2 Yes

3 $2 \times 1 = 2$, $1 \times 2 = 2$
$4 \times 1 = 4$, $2 \times 2 = 4$
$6 \times 1 = 6$, $3 \times 2 = 6$
$8 \times 1 = 8$, $4 \times 2 = 8$
$10 \times 1 = 10$, $5 \times 2 = 10$
$12 \times 1 = 12$, $6 \times 2 = 12$

4 Possible answers include:
$0 \times 1 = 0$, $1 \times 1 = 1$, $2 \times 1 = 2$,
$3 \times 1 = 3$, $4 \times 1 = 4$, $10 \times 1 = 10$,
$11 \times 1 = 11$, $12 \times 1 = 12$, $0 \times 2 = 0$,
$1 \times 2 = 2$, $2 \times 2 = 4$, $10 \times 2 = 20$,
$11 \times 2 = 22$, $12 \times 2 = 24$

5 4 £2 coins + 1 £1 coin = 5 coins
3 £2 + 3 £1 = 6 coins
2 £2 + 5 £1 = 7 coins
1 £2 + 7 £1 = 8 coins
It is not possible to have only 4 coins

6 It is the 1 times table, as the number remains unchanged when multiplied by 1.

Problem solving (1 and 2 division facts) (pages 36–37)

Test 1 $2 \div 2 = 1$, $4 \div 2 = 2$, $6 \div 2 = 3$,
$8 \div 2 = 4$, $10 \div 2 = 5$, $12 \div 2 = 6$,
$14 \div 2 = 7$, $16 \div 2 = 8$, $18 \div 2 = 9$,
$20 \div 2 = 10$, $22 \div 2 = 11$, $24 \div 2 = 12$

Test 2 2, 9, 2
1, 2, 0
6, 18, 2
8, 4, 12
2, 1, 24

1 Answers will vary.

2 Possible answers include:
$0 \div 1 = 0$, $1 \div 1 = 1$, $2 \div 1 = 2$,
$3 \div 1 = 3$, $4 \div 1 = 4$, $10 \div 1 = 10$,
$11 \div 1 = 11$, $12 \div 1 = 12$, $0 \div 2 = 0$,
$2 \div 2 = 1$, $4 \div 2 = 2$

3 Middle: $6 \div 2$, $10 \div 2$; Bottom: $8 \div 2$, $4 \div 2$

Problem solving (5 and 10 times tables) (pages 38–39)

Test 1 110, 6, 5
10, 5, 0
5, 7, 8
1, 45, 4
10, 3, 50

Test 2 20, 45, 10
15, 25, 35
40, 5, 30
Yes, totals add up to 75

1 90

2 $2 \times 5 = 10$, $1 \times 10 = 10$
$4 \times 5 = 20$, $2 \times 10 = 20$
$6 \times 5 = 30$, $3 \times 10 = 30$
$8 \times 5 = 40$, $4 \times 10 = 40$
$10 \times 5 = 50$, $5 \times 10 = 50$
$12 \times 5 = 60$, $6 \times 10 = 60$

3 $1 \rightarrow 1, 2 \rightarrow 1, 3 \rightarrow 2, 4 \rightarrow 2, 5 \rightarrow 3, 6 \rightarrow 3$,
$7 \rightarrow 4, 8 \rightarrow 4, 9 \rightarrow 5, 10 \rightarrow 5, 11 \rightarrow 6, 12 \rightarrow 6$

4 Across: 1. 35, 2. 20, 3. 45, 4. 50, 6. 15, 7. 40, 8. 90;
Down: 1. 30, 2. 25, 5. 60, 6. 10, 7. 40
3 down clue: 8×5 or 4×10
4 down clue: 11×5

5 This is the 10 times table, with C representing the digit 0.

Problem solving (5 and 10 division facts) (pages 40–41)

Test 1 $5 \div 5 = 1$, $10 \div 5 = 2$, $15 \div 5 = 3$,
$20 \div 5 = 4$, $25 \div 5 = 5$, $30 \div 5 = 6$,
$35 \div 5 = 7$, $40 \div 5 = 8$, $45 \div 5 = 9$,
$50 \div 5 = 10$, $55 \div 5 = 11$, $60 \div 5 = 12$

Test 2 8, 90, 5
5, 5, 0
2, 45, 10
20, 6, 120
5, 10, 60

1 $5 \times 7 = 35$, $7 \times 5 = 35$, $35 \div 5 = 7$, $35 \div 7 = 5$

2 $11 \times 10 = 110$, $10 \times 11 = 110$
$110 \div 10 = 11$, $110 \div 11 = 10$

3 No, e.g. 35 is not a multiple of 10.

4 $9 \times 5p$ = 9 stamps
$1 \times 10p + 7 \times 5p$ = 8 stamps
$2 \times 10p + 5 \times 5p$ = 7 stamps
$3 \times 10p + 3 \times 5p$ = 6 stamps
$4 \times 10p + 1 \times 5p$ = 5 stamps

5 Middle: $15 \div 5$, $25 \div 5$, $70 \div 10$,
Bottom: $16 \div 2$, $60 \div 10$

Problem solving (1, 2, 5 and 10 times tables) (pages 42–43)

Test 1 2×5, 5×2, 10×1
5×8, 8×5, 10×4
6×5, 5×6, 3×10
12×5, 5×12, 6×10

Test 2 11, 12, 5
12, 5, 0
14, 7, 10
1, 18, 4
10, 9, 60

1 50, 0, 25, 0

2 25

3 1×20, 2×10, 4×5, 5×4, 10×2, 20×1

4 1st grid top row 12, bottom row 50.
2nd grid top row 14, bottom row 55.
1st arrow 5×3; 2nd arrow 9×5

5 There are more than 28 possible solutions.

Problem solving (1, 2, 5 and 10 division facts) (pages 44–45)

Test 1

$90 \div 10$	$0 \div 10$	$50 \div 10$	$40 \div 5$	$14 \div 2$
$35 \div 5$	$12 \div 2$	$30 \div 5$	$20 \div 2$	$100 \div 10$
$45 \div 5$	$25 \div 5$	$18 \div 2$	$5 \div 5$	$0 \div 2$
$20 \div 10$	$3 \div 1$	$30 \div 10$	$1 \div 1$	$80 \div 10$
$15 \div 5$	$60 \div 10$	$16 \div 2$	$10 \div 5$	$50 \div 5$
$4 \div 2$	$40 \div 10$	$20 \div 5$	$8 \div 2$	$70 \div 10$

Test 2 11, 70, 2
9, 16, 0
40, 11, 60
2, 10, 24

1 $10 \times 5p$, $5 \times 2p$

2 110

3 There are more than 25 possible solutions.

4 Across: 1. 12, 2. 14, 3. 22, 4. 15, 6. 50, 7. 30.
Down: 1. 11, 2. 12, 3. 25, 4. 10, 5. 40, 6. 55,
7. 35
6 across clue: 5×10
7 across clue: 10×3 or 6×5

48

CUT HERE